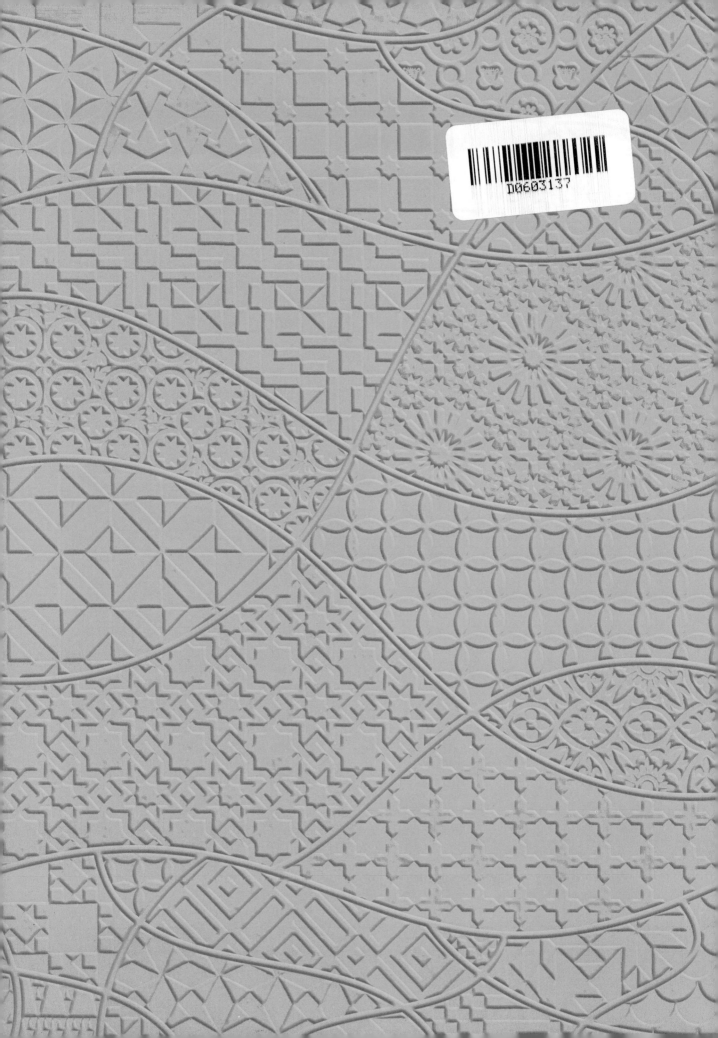

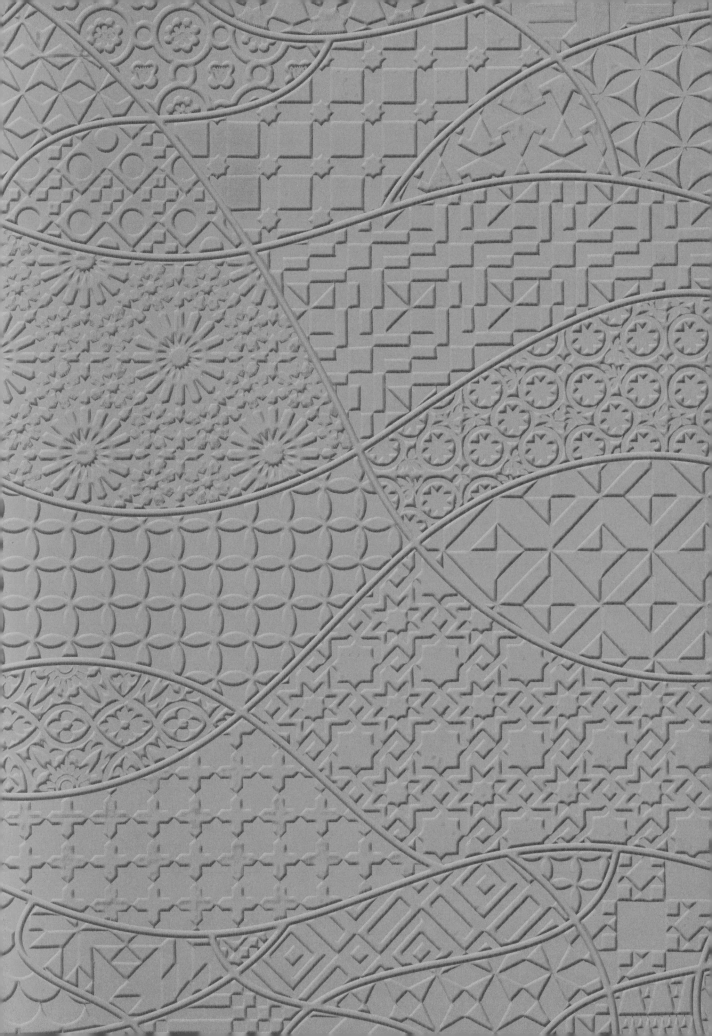

# Avenues

Alfredo Schifini
Deborah J. Short
Josefina Villamil Tinajero

Erminda García
Eugene E. García
Else Hamayan
Lada Kratky

HAMPTON-BROWN

# Grades 1–2 Curriculum Reviewers

**Kimberly L. Barto**
*Teacher*
Austin Parkway Elementary
Fort Bend Independent School District
Sugar Land, Texas

**Cynthia Cantú**
*Bilingual Teacher*
Eli Whitney Elementary
Pharr-San Juan-Alamo School District
Pharr, Texas

**Barbara Ann Genovese-Fraracci**
*District Program Specialist*
Instructional Services Center
Hacienda La Puente Unified
    School District
Hacienda Heights, California

**Robin Herrera-Snitofsky**
*Language Arts Coordinator*
Neff Elementary
Houston Independent School District
Houston, Texas

**Lizabeth Lepovitz**
*Bilingual Teacher*
James L. Carson Elementary
Northside Independent School District
San Antonio, Texas

**Derek Lewis**
*ESOL Teacher*
Bryant Woods Elementary
Howard County Public Schools
Columbia, Maryland

**Susan Mayberger**
*Supervisor of ESL*
Omaha Public Schools
Omaha, Nebraska

**Dr. Mark R. O'Shea**
*Professor of Education*
Institute for Field-Based Teacher
    Education
California State University,
    Monterey Bay
Monterey, California

**Jessica C. Rodriguez**
*Bilingual Teacher*
Manuel Jara Elementary
Fort Worth Independent
    School District
Fort Worth, Texas

**Rita C. Seru**
*Bilingual Teacher*
Thomas Gardner School
Boston Public Schools
Boston, Massachusetts

**Liz Wolfe**
*Coordinator*
Curriculum Services for
    English Learners
San Mateo County Office of
    Education
San Mateo, California

**Ruth Woods**
*ESL Teacher*
Lyndale Community School
Minneapolis Public Schools
Minneapolis, Minnesota

# Acknowledgments

Every effort has been made to secure permission, but if any omissions have been made, please let us know. We gratefully acknowledge the following permissions:

**Cover Design and Art Direction:** Pronk&Associates.

**Cover Illustration:** Maya Gonzalez.

**Creative Teaching Press:** *Round and Round the Seasons Go* © 1994 Creative Teaching Press, Inc., Huntington Beach, CA.

**Acknowledgments continue on page 185.**

Hampton-Brown
P.O. Box 223220
Carmel, California 93922
800-333-3510
www.hampton-brown.com

Printed in the United States of America

ISBN 0-7362-1825-4

04 05 06 07 08 09 10 11 12  9 8 7 6 5 4 3 2

Copyright © 2004 Hampton-Brown

Avenues Go Everywhere

# Unit 1

## What's New with You?

**Science**
- Seasons
- Growing and Changing

Unit 1 Launch . . . . . . . . . . . . . . . . . . . 6

Unit 1 Science Words . . . . . . . . . . . . . 8

**Fiction**
Realistic Fiction

**Daniel's First Day** . . . . . . . . . . **12**
by Alma Flor Ada

Vocabulary: Song . . . . . . . . . . . . . . . . . 10

Think and Respond . . . . . . Strategy: Find Details . . . . . . . 28

Content Connections . . . . . . . . . . . . . . . . 30

   Listening/Speaking: Play Simon Says

   Social Studies: Make a Class Map

   Math: Make a Feelings Graph

   Writing: Make a Photo Stick

Comprehension Skill . . . . . Details . . . . . . . . . . . . . 32

**Poetry**

**Around the Seasons** . . . . . . . . . . **36**
by Rozanne Lanczak Williams

Vocabulary: Picture Story . . . . . . . . . . . 34

Think and Respond . . . . . . Strategy: Classify Details . . . . . 54

Content Connections . . . . . . . . . . . . . . . . 56

   Listening/Speaking: Make a Seasons Movie

   Social Studies: Dress a Puppet

   Science: Match Seeds to Plants

   Writing: Make a Leaf Book

Language Skill . . . . . . . . . . Naming Words . . . . . . . . . . . 58

Unit 1 Wrap-Up . . . . . . . . . . . . . . . . . 60

# Here Come the Animals!

**Science**
- Animal Features
- Animal Behavior

**Unit 2 Launch** . . . . . . . . . . . . . . . . . . . . 62

**Unit 2 Science Words** . . . . . . . . . . . . . 64

**Fiction**
**Animal Fantasy**

**Are You an Elephant?** . . . . . . . . . . . . **68**
by Lada Kratky

    **Vocabulary:** Role-Play . . . . . . . . . . . . . . . . 66

    **Think and Respond** . . . . . . **Strategy: Sequence** . . . . . . . . 86

    **Content Connections** . . . . . . . . . . . . . . . . . . . . . 88

      **Listening/Speaking:** Play a Name Game

      **Math:** Make a Pet Graph

      **Science:** Make a Chart

      **Writing:** Make a Baby Animal Page

    **Comprehension Skill** . . . . . **Sequence** . . . . . . . . . . . . . . 90

**Nonfiction**
**Fact Book**

**Feathers and More** . . . . . . . . . . . . . . . **94**
by Barbara Wood

    **Vocabulary:** Song . . . . . . . . . . . . . . . . . . . . . 92

    **Think and Respond** . . . . . . **Strategy: Classify** . . . . . . . . 106

    **Content Connections** . . . . . . . . . . . . . . . . . . . . 108

      **Listening/Speaking:** Play a Game

      **Math:** Sort Animals

      **Science:** Make an Animal Home

      **Writing:** Make an Animal Poster

    **Language Skill** . . . . . . . . . **Action Words** . . . . . . . . . . 110

**Unit 2 Wrap-Up** . . . . . . . . . . . . . . . . 112

# Unit 3

## Families on the Go

**Social Studies**
- Families
- Culture

Unit 3 Launch . . . . . . . . . . . . . . . . . . . 114

Unit 3 Social Studies Words . . . . . . . . 116

**Fiction**
Realistic Fiction

### Dim Sum for Everyone! . . . . . . . . . . . . . . **120**
by Grace Lin

Vocabulary: Role-Play . . . . . . . . . . . . . . . 118

Think and Respond . . . . . . Strategy: Sequence . . . . . . . 142

Content Connections . . . . . . . . . . . . . . . . . . . . 144

   Listening/Speaking: Talk About Your Favorite Dinner

   Math: Count the People

   Social Studies: Learn About Rice

   Writing: Write an Invitation

Comprehension Skill . . . . . Main Idea . . . . . . . . . . . 146

**Nonfiction**
Photo Book

### Families . . . . . . . . . . . . . . . . . . . . . . . . **150**
by Ann Morris

Vocabulary: Song . . . . . . . . . . . . . . . . . . . . . 148

### Spin . . . . . . . . . . . . . . . . . . . . . . . . . . . . 168
Poem by Angela Johnson

Think and Respond . . . . . . Strategy: Main Idea and Details . 170

Content Connections . . . . . . . . . . . . . . . . . . . . 172

   Listening/Speaking: Listen to a Guest Speaker

   Art: Make a Locket

   Social Studies: Make a List of Chores

   Writing: Make a Photo Book

Language Skill . . . . . . . . . Pronouns: *he, she, it* and *they* . . . 174

Unit 3 Wrap-Up . . . . . . . . . . . . . . 176

Picture Dictionary . . . . . . . . . . . . . . . . . . . . . . . . . . 178

# What's New with You?

## Show What You Can Do

1. Draw a picture of something new you can do.
2. Act it out for a group.

# Seasons and Weather

**Spring**

red flower

little pot

warm and rainy

**Summer**

hot and sunny

## Fall

cool and windy

## Winter

cold and snowy

Song

# Time for School

Time **for** **me**

To go to school.

I will learn about

Something **new**.

Tune: "Jack, Be Nimble"

## New Words

for

me

new

# Daniel's First Day

by Alma Flor Ada

illustrated by Joe Cepeda

# Read a Story

**Who is in the story?**

Daniel

Daniel's friends

teacher

**Where does this story happen?**

at school

Selection Reading

new clothes for me

new school for me

new work for me

new food for me

new games for me

new words for me

new friends for me

## Meet the Author
# Alma Flor Ada

AWARD WINNER

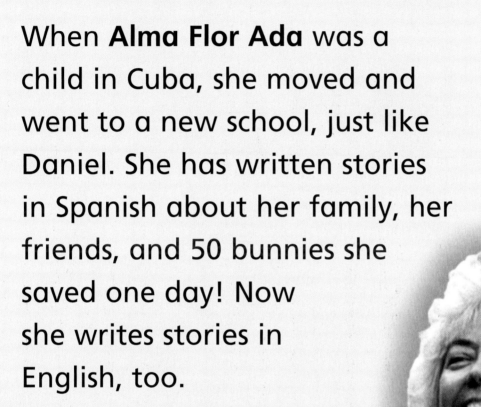

When **Alma Flor Ada** was a child in Cuba, she moved and went to a new school, just like Daniel. She has written stories in Spanish about her family, her friends, and 50 bunnies she saved one day! Now she writes stories in English, too.

# Think and Respond

## Strategy: Find Details

What are Daniel's new things?

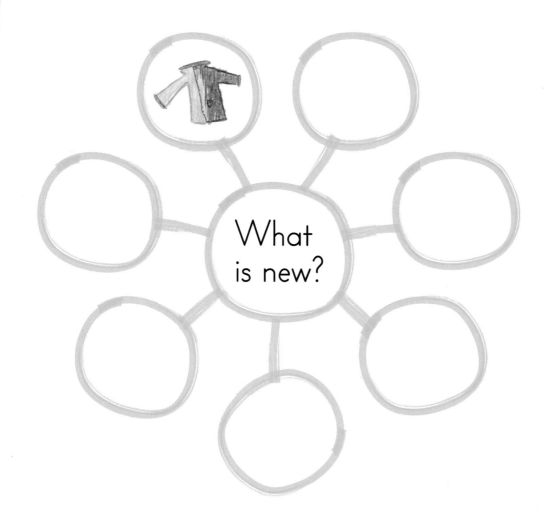

**What is new?**

## Retell the Story

Work with a partner.

Use the web.

Tell what is new for Daniel.

## Talk It Over

**1** What is Daniel's first day of school like?

What was your first day of school like?

**2** Name three things Daniel learns.

**3** How does Daniel feel at the end of the story?

# Content Connections

LISTENING/
SPEAKING

## Play Simon Says

small group

1. Be the teacher.

2. Give directions to
   play the game.

Raise your hand.

SOCIAL
STUDIES

## Make a Class Map

**Internet**

large group

What country is your family from?

1. Find the country's flag.

2. Make a card with the
   flag and your name.

3. Put your card on the map.
   Tell where you are from.

Sali

## Make a Feelings Graph

large group

1. Draw a face on a paper plate.

2. Act out your feelings on the first day of school.

3. Use all the plates to make a feelings graph.

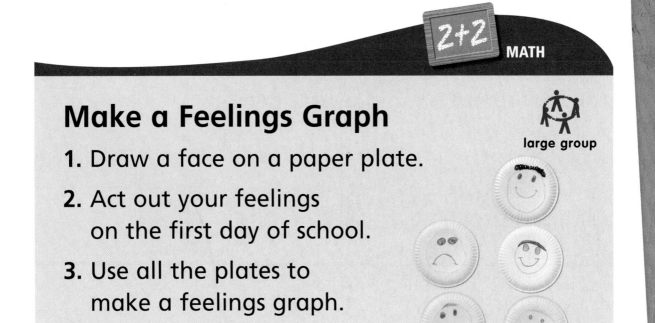

## Make a Photo Stick

on your own

1. Bring a baby picture from home.

2. Bring a picture of you now.

3. Write your name and age.

4. Use your stick. Talk about yourself then and now.

# Details

When you read, look for **details** .
Details tell about an important idea.

Important Idea

Detail   Detail   Detail

What is one detail in this story?

## A New Sweater

Su Hee wants a new sweater. One detail is that it is blue.

Su Hee wants a new sweater. She and her mother go to the store. Su Hee picks a pretty sweater. It is blue. It is soft. She loves her new sweater!

# Practice

Take this test. Find the **detail**.

**✔ Test Tip**

Always start with the directions.

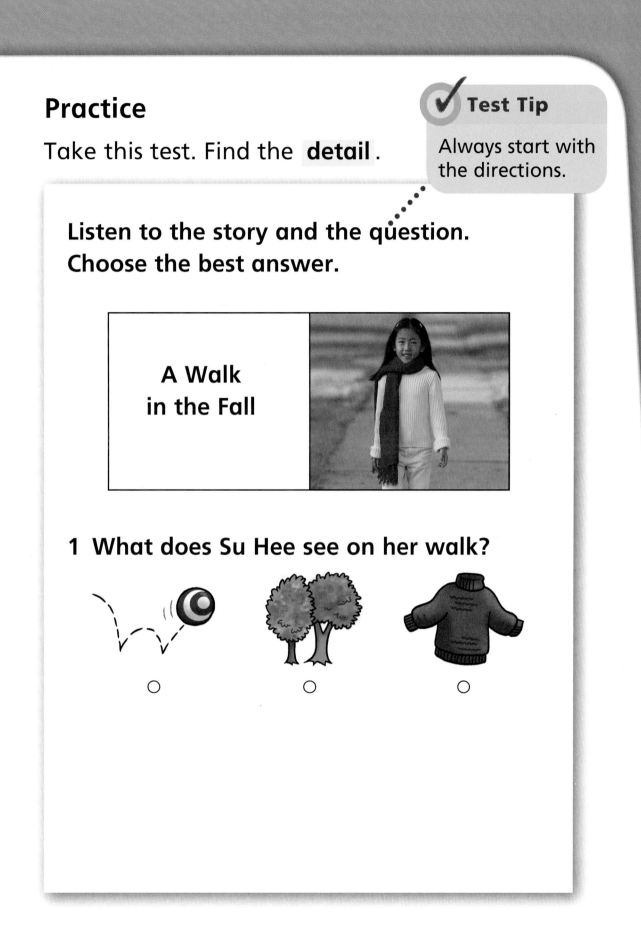

**Listen to the story and the question. Choose the best answer.**

A Walk in the Fall

**1 What does Su Hee see on her walk?**

○          ○          ○

# Nadia's Year

**Fall**

I **go** to school.
I wear a jacket.

**Winter**

It is **cold** outside.
I play in the snow.

**Spring**

The rain **comes** down.
My flowers grow.

## New Words

go

cold

comes

hot

and

**Summer**

It is **hot**!
I run **and** play outside.

# Read a Seasons Poem

Many poems have words that **rhyme**, or end with the same sounds.

✔ Listen for rhyming words.

Round and round

the seasons **go**.

Winter comes,

cold, white **snow**.

**These words rhyme.**

🔘 **Selection Reading**

# Around the Seasons

by Rozanne Lanczak Williams

illustrated by Claudine Gèvry

# Round and round

the seasons go.

Winter comes,

cold, white snow.

# Round and round

the seasons go.

Spring comes,

flowers grow.

# Round and round

the seasons go.

Summer comes,

hot and slow.

# Round and round

the seasons go.

Fall comes,

leaves blow!

# Think and Respond

## Strategy: Classify Details

What is each season like?

What do you do in each season?

### Around the Seasons

| Season | What Is It Like? | What Can You Do? |
|--------|------------------|-------------------|
| winter | | |
| spring | | |
| summer | | |
| fall | | |

## Talk About the Seasons

Use the chart.

Talk about the seasons.

Tell what you do in each season.

## Talk It Over

**1** What season comes after spring?

**2** Name two things you can do outside in the winter.

**3** Look at the stories from this unit.

What things change in these stories?

The seasons change in "Around the Seasons."

# Content Connections

## Make a Seasons Movie

small group

1. Draw each season.

2. Write a caption about it.

3. Make a movie.

4. Talk about the seasons.

Summer is hot.

SOCIAL
STUDIES

## Dress a Puppet

It is cold. My puppet wears a coat.

partners

1. Make a puppet and some clothes.

2. Dress your puppet.

3. Tell what the weather is like. Tell what the puppet is wearing.

## Match Seeds to Plants

**Internet**

partners

1. Find out about seeds and plants.

2. Draw a fruit or vegetable. Draw its seed.

3. Talk about your drawing.

WRITING

## Make a Leaf Book

partners

1. Find a leaf.

2. Put your leaf on a page.

3. Write about it.

4. Put your page in a class book.

a red leaf

# Naming Words

**Listen and sing.**

Song

# Spring

Winter turns to spring.
Flowers start to grow.
Say hello to sunny days.
Say goodbye to snow!

Tune: "The Farmer in the Dell"

## Let's Learn!

**Naming words** name a person, animal, place, or thing.

| Person | Animal | Place | Thing |
|--------|--------|-------|-------|
| friend | dog | home | flower |
| boy | cat | school | snow |

## Let's Talk!

Point to something in the classroom.

Ask a friend to name it.

chair

## Let's Write!

Draw a picture on a card.

Name it on another card.

Mix up the cards and match them.

flower

# Show What You Know

## Talk About Seasons

Look back at the stories.

What do they show about the seasons?

Make a chart.

| Fall | Winter | Spring | Summer |
|------|--------|--------|--------|
| rake leaves | snow | | |

## Share Your Work

Draw a picture of a season.

Tell what you like about it.

Put your picture in a class book.

# Read and Learn More

## Leveled Books

**At School**
by Lada Kratky

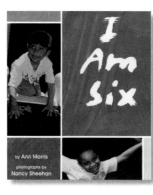

**I Am Six**
by Ann Morris

## Theme Library

**Fall Leaves Fall!**
by Zoe Hall

**Growing Colors**
by Bruce McMillan

Internet
Go to: www.hbavenues.com

Weather Fun

Seasons

Paint a Picture

# Here Come the Animals!

## What Animal Am I?

1. Work with a group. Pick an animal.
2. Act out the animal.
3. Have the group find the card for your animal.

# Animal Names and Body Parts

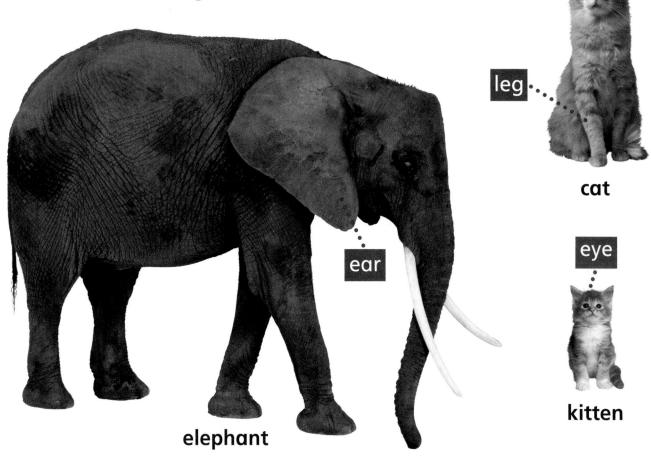

leg

cat

eye

kitten

ear

elephant

wing

beak

bird

nose

tail

paw

dog

# Animal Coverings

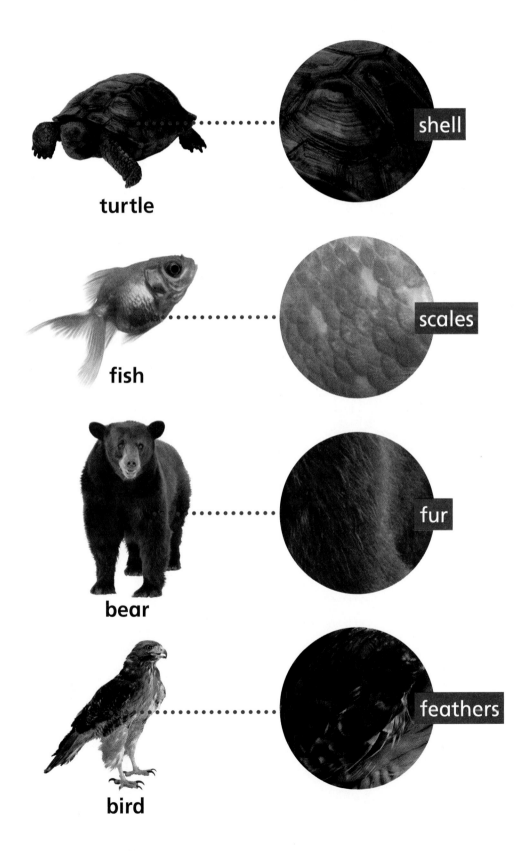

turtle — shell

fish — scales

bear — fur

bird — feathers

Are You an Elephant?

# Vocabulary

# What Animal Are You?

Act out the interview.

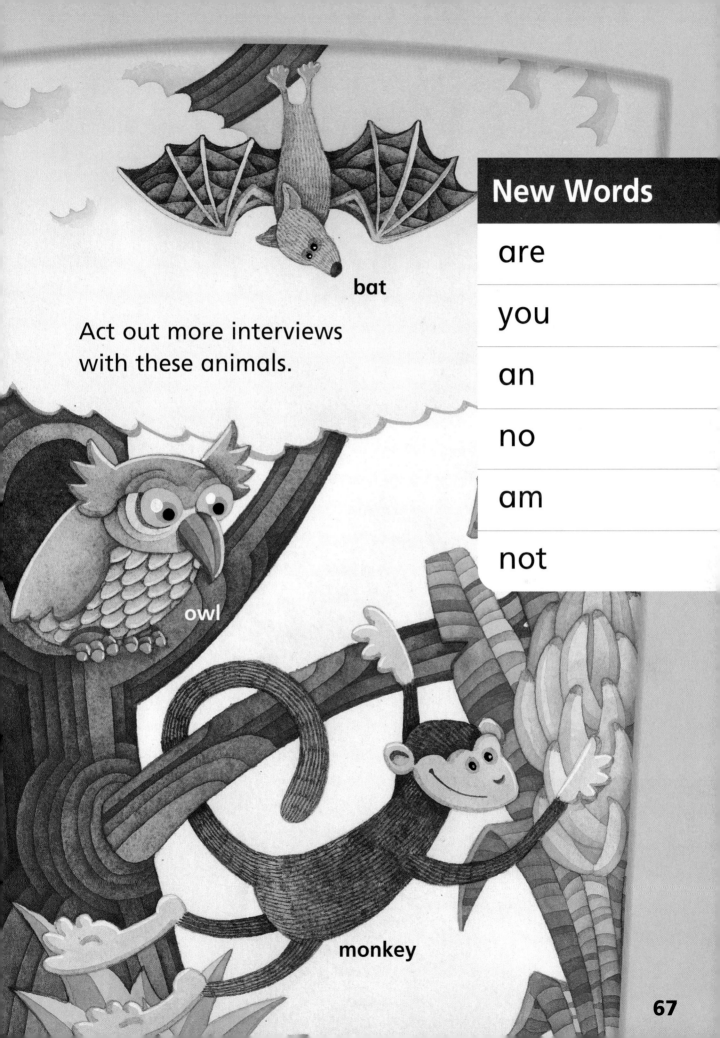

bat

Act out more interviews with these animals.

owl

monkey

## New Words

are

you

an

no

am

not

# Are You an Elephant?

by Lada Kratky

illustrated by
Wayne Parmenter

# Read a Story

**Who is in the story?**

owl

bat

elephant

monkey

parrot

Selection Reading

# Are you an elephant?

No, I am not.
I am an owl.

Are you an elephant?

No, I am not.
I am a bat.

Are you an elephant?

No, I am not.
I am a parrot.

Are you an elephant?

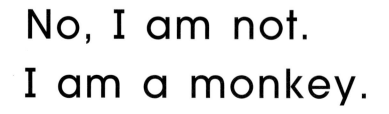

No, I am not.
I am a monkey.

Are you an elephant?

Yes, I am an elephant!

I am your dad!

## Meet the Author

# Lada Kratky

**Lada Kratky** loves to write. She loves elephants, too. She has seen elephants in Africa and at the zoo. Where have you seen an elephant?

# Think and Respond

## Who Is in the Story?

The baby elephant saw a lot of animals.

Draw the animals.

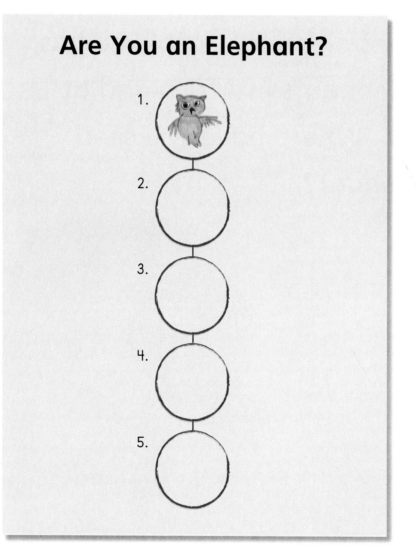

## Retell the Story

Use your story map.

Retell the story to a friend.

## Talk It Over

**1** Do you think the baby elephant is lost? Why or why not?

**2** How do you think the baby elephant feels at the end of the story?

**3** Tell another story about a baby animal. How is it different from this story?

# Content Connections

## Play a Name Game

**partners**

Play a matching game.
Match the
animal to
its baby.
Tell about
the baby.

A baby cow
is a calf.

**MATH**

2+2

## Make a Pet Graph

**large group**

1. Ask friends about their pets.
   Who has a cat?
   Who has a fish?

2. Make a graph.

3. Tell what the graph shows.
   How many cats are there?

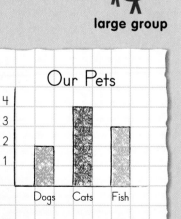

Our Pets

Dogs  Cats  Fish

## Make a Chart

1. Look around your classroom.
   What is living?
   What is nonliving?

2. Make a chart.

3. Show your chart to a group.

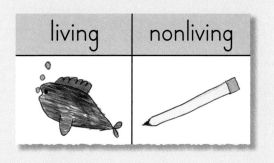

| living | nonliving |
|--------|-----------|

## Make a Baby Animal Page

**Internet**

Find out about a baby animal.

1. Print out a picture or draw a picture.

2. Write about it.

3. Tell about your animal.

The kitten is little.

# Sequence

The **sequence** is the order of events in the story.

Sequence = First + Next + Last

What is the sequence of this story?

## A Trip to the Zoo

Marta and her family go to the zoo. First, they see an elephant. Next, they see more animals. Last, they see a lion. They have fun!

First, they see an elephant. Next, they see more animals. Last, they see a lion.

# Practice

Take this test. Find the **sequence** .

**Listen to the story and the question. Choose the best answer.**

### Javier's Pet

Javier wants a pet. First, he reads books about pets. Next, his mother takes him to the pet store. Last, he picks a blue fish. He likes his pet!

**1  What happens in the middle of the story?**

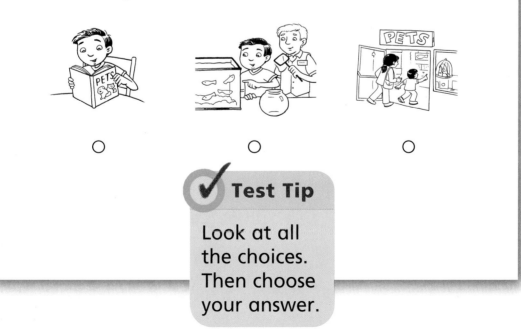

○              ○              ○

**✓ Test Tip**

Look at all the choices. Then choose your answer.

# Vocabulary

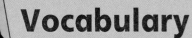

Song

# My New Cat

My cat **has** fur.

Do you know why?

It **keeps** her **warm**

and safe and dry.

She has **a** face

so soft and sweet.

I **help** her play

and sleep and eat!

Tune: "Twinkle, Twinkle, Little Star"

## New Words

has

keeps

warm

a

help

# Read a Fact Book

A **fact book** is nonfiction.

It tells about things that are real.

✔ Look for **facts**.

✔ Look for **labels**.

feathers

**A bird has feathers.** a fact

# Feathers and More

## by Barbara Wood

A bird has feathers.

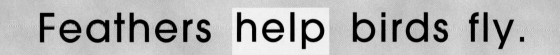

Feathers **help** birds fly.

fur

A dog has fur.

Fur keeps dogs warm.

shell

A turtle has a shell.

Shells keep turtles safe.

scales

Fish have scales.

Scales help fish move
in the water.

hen

Look at
more animals.

crab

tiger

snake

Do they have feathers, fur, shells, or scales?

# Think and Respond

## Strategy: Classify

Look at "Feathers and More" again.

What animal goes in each box?

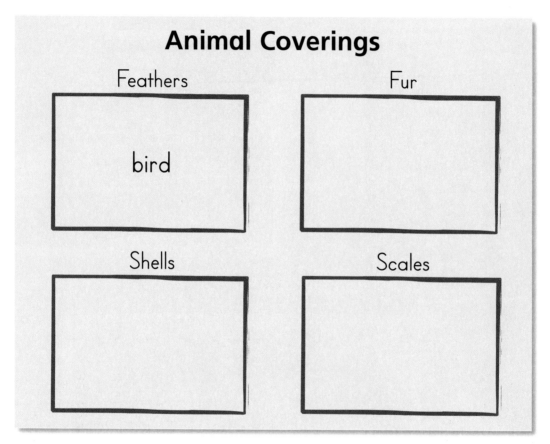

**Animal Coverings**

Feathers

bird

Fur

Shells

Scales

## Tell About the Animals

Use the chart.

Tell how two animals are alike.

## Talk It Over

1 Tell one thing you learned about animals.

2 Why do shells keep turtles safe?

3 Look at "Are You an Elephant?" and "Feathers and More."

How are they different?

"Feathers and More" has facts about animals.

# Content Connections

## Play a Game

**large group**

1. Give clues about an animal.

2. Ask your friends to guess the animal.

> It has feathers.
> It can fly.
> It is green.
> What animal is it?

**MATH**

2+2

## Sort Animals

**partners**

1. Look at pictures of animals.

2. Put animals with two legs in one pile.

3. Put animals with four legs in another pile.

What other ways can you sort animals?

2 legs

4 legs

## Make an Animal Home

1. Pick an animal.

2. Make a model of the animal's home.

3. Use the model. Tell about where the animal lives.

## Make an Animal Poster

**Internet**

Work with a group. Find out about an animal. Then:

1. Draw a big picture.

2. Write two facts about it.

3. Use the poster. Tell about the animal.

A lion runs fast.
A lion has a mane.

## Action Words

**Listen and sing.**

Song

# What Do Animals Do?

The elephant walks.
The tiger runs.
The monkeys climb a tree
and sleep in the sun!

Tune: "Hot Cross Buns"

# Let's Learn!

**Action words** tell what people and animals do.

| One | More Than One |
|---|---|
| 1. Rosa jumps. | The girls jump. |
| 2. Lucas swims. | The boys swim. |
| 3. The turtle crawls. | The crabs crawl. |

# Let's Talk!

Act out an action.

Have a partner tell about the action.

Nick walks.

# Let's Write!

Tell what a friend does.

Write a sentence.

Draw a picture to go with your sentence.

Marcos swims.

## Show What You Know

### Pick Your Favorite Story

Talk about the animal stories.

Put your name under your favorite story in the class chart.

**Stories We Like**

| Mama Cat Has Three Kittens | Are You an Elephant? | Feathers and More |
|---|---|---|
| Delia | Carlos | Erminda |
| Yung | | Ada |

### Share Your Work

Show your favorite work about animals.

Tell what you like about it.

Put it in a class book.

# Read and Learn More

**Leveled Books**

**Say Hello!**
by Sheron Long

**I See Tails!**
by Lada Kratky

**Theme Library**

**Catch That Goat!**
by Polly Alakija

**Sweet Dreams**
by Kimiko
Kajikawa

**Internet**

Go to: www.hbavenues.com

Look at Animals

Look at Birds

All About Animals

# Families on the Go

114

## Make a Paper Chain

What do you do with your family?

1. Draw your family.
2. Paste the chain.
3. Talk about the people in your family.

# Families

Meet my family.

**my great-grandma**

**my grandpa and grandma**

my brothers

my mother

my father

my sister

me

# Families Work and Play Together

cook dinner

clean the house

eat at a restaurant

celebrate

# In a Restaurant

Act out the story.

I want a bowl **of** rice.

New Words

of

little

wants

dishes

I want a **little** bowl of soup. He **wants** egg rolls.

We all want **dishes** of ice cream!

119

# Dim Sum for Everyone!

by Grace Lin

# Read a Story

**Who is in the story?**

a family

**Where does the story happen?**

in a restaurant

**What is dim sum?**

Dim sum is Chinese food on little dishes.

**Selection Reading**

Dim sum has
many little dishes.

Little dishes on carts.
Little dishes on tables.

Ma-Ma picks little dishes
of sweet pork buns.

Ba-Ba chooses little
dishes of fried shrimp.

Jie-Jie wants turnip cakes.

Mei-Mei wants sweet tofu.

I like little egg tarts.

We eat a little
bit of everything.

Everyone eats a little bit
of everything.

Now there are
empty little dishes.

## Meet the Author and Illustrator

# Grace Lin

**Grace Lin** has been writing children's books since she was in the sixth grade. The family in this story is like her family. Ms. Lin's favorite little dish is egg tarts. She says, "Anything that is strange or different can be wonderful! Give it a chance!"

# Think and Respond

## Strategy: Sequence

What happens at dinner?

Put these sentences in order.

We eat it all!    We sit.    We choose.

### Dim Sum for Everyone!

1.

2.

3.

## Retell the Story

Work in a group.

Tell what happens in the story.

## Talk It Over

**1** What do you like best about the story? Why?

**2** What is your favorite food? What is your family's favorite food?

**3** Tell how the food in this story is the same or different from the food you eat.

# Content Connections

## Talk About Your Favorite Dinner

**partners**

1. Draw your favorite dinner.
2. Show your drawing to a friend.
3. Talk about the food you like to eat.

## Count the People

**on your own**

1. Draw a family dinner at your house.
2. Draw a holiday dinner with your family.
3. Tell how many people are at each dinner.

5 people

# Learn About Rice

## Internet

small group

1. Find a fact about rice.

2. Make a page about rice.

3. Add your page to a class book.

Rice is gohan in Japan.

WRITING

# Write an Invitation

on your own

1. Plan a dim sum party. Think about the little dishes people can bring.

2. Make an invitation to your party.

# Main Idea

The **main idea** is the important idea in a story.
**Details** tell more about the main idea.

Main Idea = Important Idea

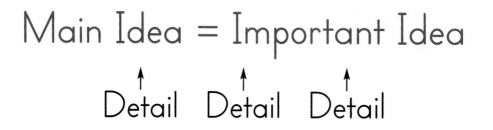

↑ ↑ ↑
Detail Detail Detail

What is the main idea in this story?

## A Family Meal

Everyone in my family helps
make dinner. My mother cuts
the vegetables. My brother
makes a salad. My sister makes
the dessert.

The main idea is
that everyone helps
make dinner.

# Practice

Take this test. Find the **main idea**.

**Listen to the story and the question. Choose the best answer.**

### What Emily Likes

Emily likes to cook. She makes cookies with her mom. She makes pizza with her dad. She makes salad all by herself. Emily has fun!

**1 What is the main idea of the story?**

- ○ Emily makes salad by herself.
- ○ Emily makes pizza with her dad.
- ○ Emily likes to cook.

✓ **Test Tip**

Do you know the answer? If you don't, read the story again.

Song

# Family

I can see

It's nice to be

**Part** of a **family** .

We all love our families.

In **work** or **play**

**They** each find a way

To be close **together**

As one family.

Tune: "Dear Old Pals"

**148**

part

family

work

play

they

together

149

# Read a Photo Book

A **photo book** uses photos to tell about something.

photo

✔ Think about what the photos show.

 Selection Reading

# Families

by Ann Morris

Everyone,

everywhere,

is **part** of a **family**.

People in families
love and care for

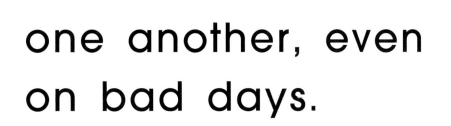

one another, even
on bad days.

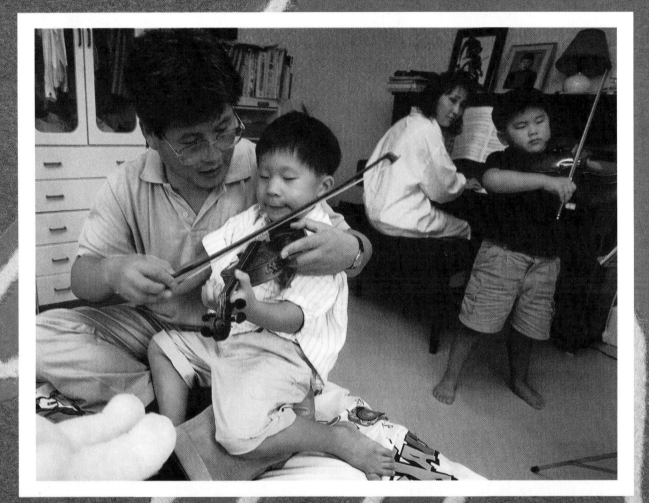

They help one another.

They work together.

They play together.

They cook,

and eat,

and celebrate together.

Whether you go to lands near or far, families are there—big and small.

Families are
loving, sharing,
and caring,

wherever you are.

# Spin

Spin around the room.

Spin around the tree.

Swirl

Twirl

Spin and twist

Big sister and me.

—*Angela Johnson*

AWARD WINNER

## Meet the Poet

**Angela Johnson** decided to be a writer when she was little. Her father and grandfather always shared stories with her. Now she writes stories and poems for you!

# Think and Respond

## Strategy: Main Idea and Details

Find the main idea in the story.

Then find the details.

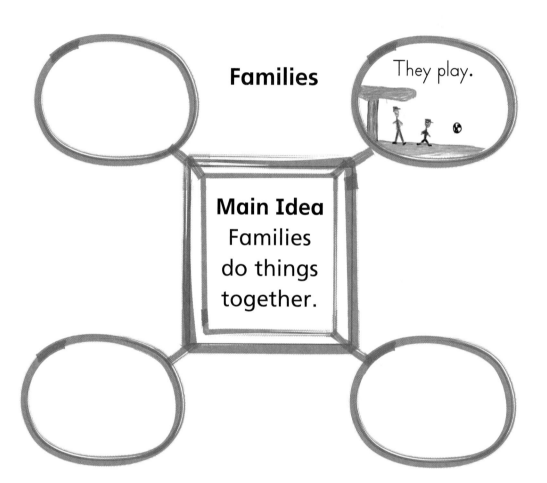

**Families**

They play.

**Main Idea**
Families
do things
together.

## Talk About the Main Idea

Use your chart.

Tell a partner about things
families do together.

## Talk It Over

**1** What will you tell a friend about the photo story?

**2** What is your favorite photo from the story? Why?

**3** Pick a photo or picture from one of the stories. Compare it to your family.

My family likes to play music, too.

# Content Connections

LISTENING/ SPEAKING

## Listen to a Guest Speaker

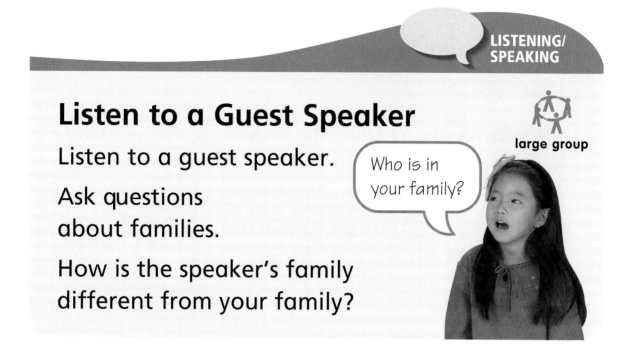

large group

Listen to a guest speaker.

Who is in your family?

Ask questions about families.

How is the speaker's family different from your family?

ART

## Make a Locket

on your own

1. Cut out a locket.

2. Draw a picture of a family member inside.

3. Tell about your locket.

my mom

# Make a List of Chores

small group

1. Write the names of people in your family.

2. List the chores each person does.

3. Talk about the chores you do.

Family Chores
me – feed the rabbit
Juan – make the beds
Mom – sweep the floor
Dad – wash the dishes

# Make a Photo Book

**Internet**

China

In China, people eat wonton soup.

1. Find out about the foods families eat around the world.

2. Make a page for a class photo book about food.

3. Write a note for your page.

small group

# He, She, It, and They

**Listen and sing.**

Song

# Mom and Dad

When Dad's in the kitchen
He helps Mom bake.
See how they talk
and they laugh.

When Mom's in the garden
She helps Dad rake.
Oh, how they talk
and they laugh.

Tune: "Come to the Fair"

# Let's Learn!

**He**, **she**, **it**, and **they** can take the place of a naming word.

| <u>He</u> and <u>They</u> | <u>She</u> and <u>It</u> |
|---|---|
| 1. **Tom** eats. <br> ↓ <br> **He** eats. | 2. **Mother** eats. <br> ↓ <br> **She** eats. |
| 3. **The girls** eat. <br> ↓ <br> **They** eat. | 4. **The dish** is empty. <br> ↓ <br> **It** is empty. |

# Let's Talk!

Tell what a partner does.

Say the sentence again with <u>he</u> or <u>she</u>.

Kim sits.
She sits.

# <u>Let's Write!</u>

Write a sentence about someone in your family.

Use <u>he</u> or <u>she</u>.

Draw a picture.

She washes dishes.

## Show What You Know

### Talk About Families

What do families do together?

Vote on your favorite activity.

Put your name in a box.

**Family Fun**

| Eat Together | Go On Vacation | Play Together | Celebrate |
|---|---|---|---|
| Luis | Julia | Chin | Sara |
|  |  |  |  |

### Share Your Work

Draw a picture of your family.

Tell about what you do together.

# Read and Learn More

## Leveled Books

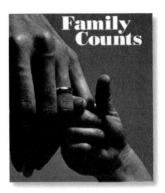

**Family Counts**
by Lada Kratky

**Dad and I**
by Liz Garza-Williams

## Theme Library

**Let's Eat!**
by Ana Zamorano

**Lots of Grandparents**
by Shelley Rotner
and Sheila Kelly

**Internet**

Go to: www.hbavenues.com

Make a Meal

Traditions

Dinner Time!

A B C D E F G H I J K L M N O P Q R S T U V W X Y Z

## A

### a

He has **a** dog.
The dog has
**a** collar.

dog

collar

### all

They wash
**all** the
dishes.

dishes

### am

I **am** Janay.

Janay

### an

I have **an** apple.

### and

I have a ball
**and** a bat.

bat

ball

### are

They **are** boys.

## B

### but

This hat is pretty,
**but** it is big!

## C

# cold

I am **cold**!

snow

ice

# comes

Here **comes** my friend!

friend

## D

# different

The shoelaces are **different** colors.

shoelaces

# dishes

There is food on these **dishes**.

dishes

## F

# family

There are seven people in this **family**.

# for

This letter is **for** Vera.

letter

Cano

Vera Cano

Vera

## G

# go

We **go** outside at recess.

a b c d e f g h i j k l m n o p q r s t u v w x y z

**179**

A B C D E F G H I J K L M N O P Q R S T U V W X Y Z

## H

### has

He **has** a toy truck.

truck

### help

The tugboats **help** the ship come into the harbor.

ship

tugboat

### her

❶ The mother hugs **her** baby.

mother

baby

❷ Marta is Thu's friend.
Marta sends **her** an E-mail.

Marta

E-mail

Thu

### hot

I am **hot**!

## I

### in

David is **in** the sandbox.

sandbox

David

### is

The balloon **is** blue.

## K

### keeps

umbrella

An umbrella **keeps** you dry in the rain.

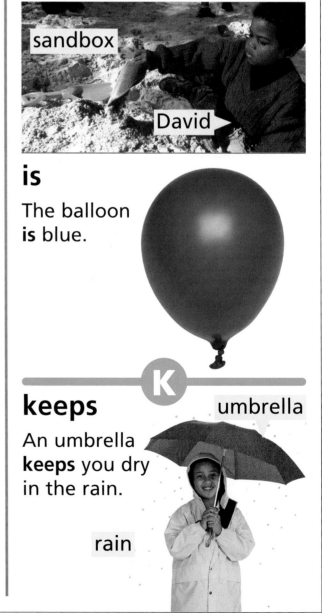

rain

## L

### little

Jeff eats a **little** bit of pudding.

a lot

a little

## M

### made

This winter Mom and I **made** a quilt.

quilt

### me

Please give the pencil to **me**.

### my

This is **my** paper.

paper

Sally

## N

### new

This boy has **new** shoes.

shoe

### no

Is this a dog? **No**, it is a cat.

### not

I am **not** sad. I am happy.

## O

### of

This is the rocking chair **of** my grandfather.

rocking chair

a b c d e f g h i j k l m n o p q r s t u v w x y z

## on

The cat is **on** the roof!

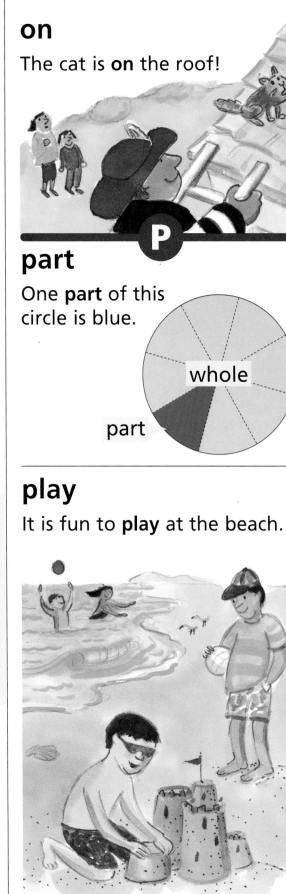

## part

One **part** of this circle is blue.

part

whole

## play

It is fun to **play** at the beach.

## same

Alexa and I have the **same** kind of cap.

caps

me

## their

Celia and Josie do **their** homework.

## then

I do my homework first. **Then** I watch TV.

homework

TV

## they

The boys have fun. **They** ride their bikes.

helmet

bike

## time

I wear my helmet every **time** I ride my bike.

on Saturday

on Tuesday

## together

These people skate **together**.

ice

## W

## wants

This man **wants** some ice cream.

## warm

These cookies are **warm**.

oven

cookies

## was

The puppy **was** small. Now it is big.

small puppy

big puppy

a b c d e f g h i j k l m n o p q r s t u v w x y z

183

## work

These students **work**.

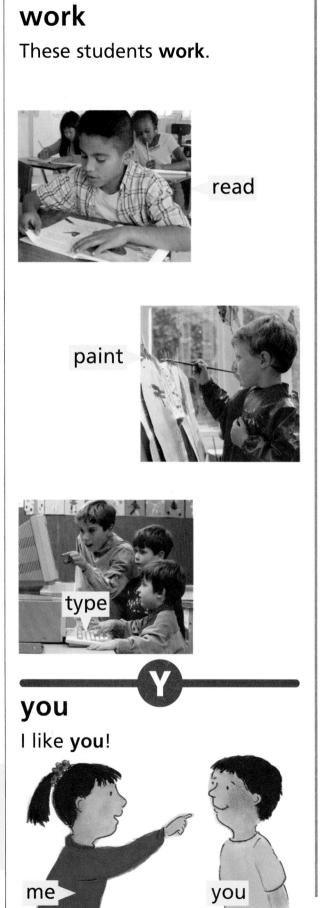

read

paint

type

**Y**

## you

I like **you**!

me    you

## Acknowledgments continued

**HarperCollins Publishers:** *Families* by Ann Morris. Used by permission of HarperCollins Publishers.

**Orchard Books, a division of Scholastic, Inc.:** "Spin" from *Daddy Calls Me Man* by Angela Johnson, illustrated by Rhonda Mitchell. Published by Orchard Books, an imprint of Scholastic Inc. Text copyright © 1997 by Angela Johnson, illustrations copyright © 1997 by Rhonda Mitchell. Reprinted by permission.

**Random House:** *Dim Sum for Everyone!* Copyright © 2001 by Grace Lin. Published by arrangement with Random House Children's Books a division of Random House, Inc., New York, New York, U.S.A. All rights reserved.

### Photographs:
**P93:** courtesy of Frances Meyer, Inc., © Ronnie for FMI (stickers).

**P116:** courtesy of the Aceves Family (grandmother and grandfather).

**George Ancona:** p157 (family).

**Bruce Coleman, Inc.:** p65 (fish scales, © Paul D Miles, Jr), p101 (dog and turtle, © Alan Blank), p105 (crab, © Norman Owen Tomalin), p108 (turtle, © Laura Riley).

**CORBIS:** (all © CORBIS) p5 (family, © Ariel Skelley), p63 (lion), p94 and 97 (hummingbird), pp100-101 (boy and turtle, © Ariel Skelley), p105 (tiger), p108 (grizzly bear), pp114-115 (family, © Ariel Skelley), p117 (mother and son, © Ariel Skelley), p121 (restaurant, © Earl & Nazima Kowall and Dim Sum, © Nik Wheeler), p146 (family cooking, © Tom & Dee Ann McCarthy), pp148-149 (family, © Tom & Dee Ann McCarthy), p163 (family eating © DigitalStock), p180 (mother and son, © Tom & Dee Ann McCarthy).

**Corel:** p103 (fish).

**Digital Studios:** p173 (soup).

**Digital Vision:** p180 (boy with truck).

**Getty Images, Inc.:** (all © Getty Images, Inc.) p4 (hen, © PhotoDisc ), p57 (leaf, © PhotoDisc), p64 (hawk, dog, cat, elephant and kitten, © PhotoDisc), p65 (bear, fur, turtle, shell, goldfish, hawk and feathers, © PhotoDisc), p88 (cow, © PhotoDisc), p89 (kitten, © PhotoDisc), p95 (hen, © PhotoDisc), pp98-99 (boy and dog, © Steve Niedorf Photography/The Image Bank), p99 (dog in snow, © Tom Stock/ Stone), p102 (magnified fish, © PhotoDisc), pp104-105 (hen, © PhotoDisc), p108 (owl, © PhotoDisc and duck, © Mary Clay/Taxi), p158 (grandmother teaching weaving, © Paul Chesley/Stone), p164 (family making masks, © Lawrence Migdale/ Stone), p178 (boys looking at book and girl trying on hat, © PhotoDisc), p181 (cat, © PhotoDisc and man in rocking chair, © C Squared Studios/PhotoDisc), p183 (figure skaters, © David Madison/Stone), p184 (boy painting and kids working on computer, © PhotoDisc).

**Grant Heilman Photography, Inc.:** p88 (calf, © Larry Lefever).

**Hutchison Picture Library:** p167 (family, © Andrew Hill).

**Image Club/Object Gear:** p180 (balloon).

**ImageState:** p166 (father on swings, © Frank Priegue), p179 (family, © Bill Stanton).

**New Century Graphics:** pp118-119 (photo of Chinese restaurant art).

**PhotoEdit, Inc.:** p90 (zoo, © Billy E. Barnes), p93 (girl and cat, © Myrleen Ferguson Cate), p117 (birthday party, © Bill Bachman, family at restaurant, © Myrleen Ferguson Cate and family cleaning, © Robert Brenner), p180 (boy in sandbox, © Susan Van Etten).

**Photo Researchers, Inc.:** p180 (tugboats with ship, ©Ken Cavanagh).

**PictureQuest LLC:** (all © PictureQuest) pp96-97 (boy with parakeet, © Daniel McCoy/Rainbow), pp102-103 (girl and fishbowl. © Yoav Levy/Phototake), p105 (rattlesnake, © Jeff Foott/Discovery Images), p116 (great grandma, © Peter & Georgina Bowater/Stock Connection), p182 (girls doing homework, © David Stover/Stock South).

**Ellen B. Senisi:** p5 (kids hugging grandmother), p155 (family), p156 (kids hugging grandmother).

**Alicia Sternberg:** pp92-93 (black and white cat).

**Elizabeth Garza Williams:** pp3, 6-7 (girl on bike), p7 (hand), p10 (girl), pp10-11 (school), p11 (teacher and students), p30 (boy), p32 (girl and mother and boy), p33 (girl), p55 (kids), p56 (boy), p59 (kids), pp62-63 (boy), p63 (hand), p88 (boy), p90 (girl), pp92-93 (book and hands), p102 (hand with magnifying glass), p107 (kids), p108 (girl), p111 (kids), p116 (family and boy), pp118-119 (family), p145 (girl), p146 (girl), p164 (confetti), p171 (kids), p172 (girl), p175 (kids), p178 (boy and dog, girl, and girl with apple), p179 (kids eating), p180 (girls typing and boy in raincoat), p181 (kids, girl with paper, boy with shoes and girl), p182 (kids with hats), p184 (boy reading).

**The Image Works:** p179 (different shoes, © Sonda Dawes).

**Viesti Associates, Inc.:** p151 (family portrait, © Martha Cooper).

**Woodfin Camp & Associates:** p150 and p161 (family on roller coaster, © Tom Stoddart/Katz), p152 (family in front of hut, © Betty Press), p153 (family on riverboat, © Catherine Karnow), p154 (family, © Momatiuk/Eastcott), p159 (family with musical instruments, © Stephanie Maze), p160 (family cutting wood, © Michael Heron), p162 (mother and daughter cooking, © James Wilson), p165 (father taking pictures, © Mike Yamashita).

### Author and Illustrator Photos:
p27 (Alma Flor Ada, © Miriam Grossman), p85 courtesy of Lada Kratky, p141 courtesy of Grace Lin, p169 courtesy of Angela Johnson.

### Illustrations:
**Rebecca Bond:** p174 (Mom and Dad); **Karen Stormer Brooks:** p33 (ball, trees, sweater), p91 (boy with book, boys with fishbowl, boy and mother), p147 (What Emily Likes); **Joe Cepeda:** p3, pp12-27, p29 (*Daniel's First Day*); **Viví Escrivá:** p58 (Spring); **Claudine Gévry:** p3, pp36-55, p61 (*Around the Seasons*); **Peter Grosshauser:** p4, pp62-63 (Here Come the Animals! background), pp66-67 (What Animal Are You?); **Amanda Haley:** pp34-35 (Nadia's Year), p60 (girl and dog); **Grace Lin:** p5, pp120-145 (*Dim Sum for Everyone!*); **Cheryl Mendenhall:** p110 (What Do Animals Do?); **Rhonda Mitchell:** pp168-169 (Spin, courtesy of Orchard Books); **Wayne Parmenter:** p4, pp68-89 (*Are You An Elephant?*); **Roni Shepherd:** p178 (all), p179 (cold, comes, for, go), p180 (hot), p181 (little, made), p182 (on, play, then), p183 (they, time, wants, warm, was), p184 (you); **Pamela Thomson:** pp118-119 (In a Restaurant); **Suling Wang:** p8-9 (Seasons and Weather).

### The Avenues Development Team
Hampton-Brown extends special thanks to the following staff who contributed so much to the creation of the Grade 1 and 2 Pupil Editions.

**Editorial:** Renee Biermann, Susan Buntrock, Julie Cason, Honor Cline, Shirleyann Costigan, Roseann Erwin, Kristin FitzPatrick, Margot Hanis, Mary Hawley, Fredrick Ignacio, Phillip Kennedy, Dawn Liseth, Sheron Long, and Ann Seivert.

**Design and Production:** Chaos Factory and Associates, Kim Cockrum, Sherry Corley, Darius Detwiler, Jeri Gibson, Raymond Ortiz Godfrey, Delaina Hodgden, Raymond Hoffmeyer, Rick Holcomb, Leslie McDonald, Michael Moore, Andrea Pastrano-Tamez, Stephanie Rice, Augustine Rivera, Debbie Saxton, Curtis Spitler, Jonni Stains, Alicia Sternberg, Debbie Wright Swisher, Andrea Erin Thompson, Terry Taylor, Teri Wilson, and Hoshin Woo.

**Permissions:** Barbara Mathewson.